10.95

Gallery Books
Editor: Peter Fallon

THE YALTA GAME

Brian Friel

THE
YALTA
GAME

after Chekhov

Gallery Books

The Yalta Game
is first published
simultaneously in paperback
and in a clothbound edition
on the day of its première,
2 October 2001.

The Gallery Press
Loughcrew
Oldcastle
County Meath
Ireland

ISBN 1 85235 301 5 (*paperback*)
      1 85235 302 3 (*clothbound*)

    The Gallery Press acknowledges the financial assistance of An Chomhairle Ealaíon / The Arts Council, Ireland, and the Arts Council of Northern Ireland.

for Cassie

Characters

DMITRY DMITRICH GUROV, 39
ANNA SERGEYEVNA, 22

The Yalta Game was first produced in the Gate Theatre, Dublin, on Tuesday, 2 October 2001, with the following cast:

DMITRY DMITRICH GUROV   Ciarán Hinds
ANNA SERGEYEVNA   Kelly Reilly

Director	Karel Reisz
Set Designer	Eileen Diss
Costume Designer	Dany Everett
Lighting Designer	Mick Hughes
Composer	Conor Linehan
Sound Designer	John Leonard

Literal translation by Úna Ní Dhubhghaill.

The stage is furnished with a table with a circular, marble top; two or three chairs which can be used outdoors or indoors; and perhaps a couch.

DMITRY DMITRICH GUROV *is thirty-nine. His hair is beginning to turn grey. He wears his straw hat at a jaunty angle and carries a cane. He is now enjoying the late summer sun in Yalta. An exuberant military band is playing in the distance.* GUROV *listens for a few moments.*

GUROV Stirring, aren't they? Seventh Hussars from the camp over in Balaclava. (*He calls an imaginary waiter*) **Another coffee when you find a second.** (*Listens to the music again and conducts vigorously*) Make you want to charge into combat, wouldn't it?

The music begins to fade.

Believe me, when the summer season is at its height, there is no resort in the whole of the Crimea more exciting, more vibrant, than Yalta. The crowds. The bustling restaurants. The commotion of different languages. The promenade. The elegant municipal park. The obligatory day-trip to the silver waterfall at Oreanda. The nightly ritual of going down to the quay and watching the new arrivals pouring out of the Theodosia ferry with its lights dancing and expectant. And of course the mysterious Black Sea itself that embraces and holds all these elements together, especially at night when the water is a soft, warm lilac and the moon throws a shaft of gold across it. (*To the imaginary waiter*) **Thank you kindly. And sugar? Excellent.**

He now spreads out on a seat and tilts his

straw hat forward so that his eyes are almost concealed.

But of course the town square is the heart of Yalta. That's where the tourists congregate and sip coffee from morning until night. And from under their straw hats and parasols, silently, secretly, they scrutinize one another. It is the great unacknowledged Yalta game. And it is played in a kind of dream-state — and at the same time almost voraciously.

(*Softly*) That couple is back. Where were they yesterday? Not married, are they? Madam, please! Certainly not married. There's that Greek boy again. Still coughing. His eyes are so disengaged — what disappointment is he trying to recuperate from? When that husband dies this winter, as indeed he will, what will become of her? Has she the resolution to stagger on? Oh, yes, she has. Look at her staring into space — she's already making all the icy calculations.

They're new. French, are they? Has she been crying? Haven't exchanged a word all afternoon. He's clearly a prig. And his foot never stops tapping. Young lady, you shouldn't let him see how desperately you love him.

It's a day-long diversion, drinking coffee and divining other lives or investing the lives of others with an imagined life. Harmless enough, I suppose.

Madam, please! This is a public square!

You know the season is coming to an end when you see the first of the shutters going up and the wind whips up a choking dust and there is only a score of coffee-drinkers left to invent one another.

And slowly the vibrancy and excitement subside and the place becomes . . . not yet desolate but just a little dejected. And you realise you have to disengage yourself from these dreamy pleasures and this other-world routine and think about going back to Moscow — work, children, wife. (*Pause*) Home. That requires a little . . . effort.

I had been in Yalta for almost two weeks and on my second-last day, about three in the afternoon, I was sitting in the square with the remnants of the faithful. And suddenly a young woman appeared. Out of the Marino Hotel. White blouse. Grey skirt. Simple little hat. And a fawn Pomeranian at her heels. And came across the square towards our corner, walking briskly with her head down as if she wanted to be under observation for as short a time as possible.

And the straw hats and parasols stirred ever so slightly.

Enter ANNA SERGEYEVNA *with her imaginary dog. She is twenty-two. She sits and calls a waiter.*

ANNA **One coffee, please. Black.** (*To dog*) **Sit — sit.**

GUROV Now that's new. That's interesting. Twenty? Twenty-two? Not more. Russian? Oh yes. Married? Think so. Why? Instinct; and the dog maybe. Is there a husband back in the hotel? Maybe not here at all? Why not? Let's find out.

ANNA I sent my husband a telegram when I got here two days ago. 'DEAR NIKOLAI, ARRIVED SAFELY. HOTEL MARINO COMFORTABLE. WEATHER MIXED. DOING A LOT OF WALKING. GET SONIA TO

SHAMPOO ALL THE UPSTAIRS CARPETS.'

His reply came this morning. 'I MISS YOU SO BADLY BUT IT WILL BE A WONDERFUL BREAK FOR YOU. IT WILL MAKE A NEW WOMAN OF YOU. ENJOY IT. I WILL JOIN YOU JUST AS SOON AS I CAN GET AWAY. ALL MY LOVE TO MY INFANT. NIKOLAI.'

He was forty then. I could have been his 'infant'. And I could see his quiet earnest eyes as he wrote the words — he thought that being his infant must make me feel so assured. And even though the panic to get away from Pargolovo had already lost some of its urgency now that I was here, the words, 'my infant' animated that restlessness again and I had to keep telling myself that yes, Yalta would restore me, give my life some calm again, show me how much I had to be grateful for. Or at least reconcile me to what I had settled for.

GUROV **You just missed the Hussars. Trying to quicken the blood for battle.**

    Pause.

    He's a handsome little fellow.
ANNA **Yes.**
GUROV **Is he a bit spoiled?**
ANNA **She.**
GUROV *(To dog)* **I beg your pardon.**
ANNA **Birthday present from Nikolai, my husband.**
GUROV **Very nice.** *(Aside)* **Nikolai! An octogenarian with a bulbous nose — and a drip.** *(To* ANNA*)* **Has she a name?**
ANNA **Not yet.**
GUROV **Very intelligent eyes. Understanding. May I give her a biscuit?**

ANNA   If you wish.

GUROV   Here, girl. (*Withdraws his hand quickly*) Hey, I'm only being agreeable.

ANNA   She's nervous.

GUROV   I'm not going to harm you. (*Pause*) First time in Yalta?

ANNA   Yes.

GUROV   You'll be back. I come every year; part holiday, part work. (*Pause*) I'm an accountant in a bank. (*Brief pause*) Although I did my degree in philology. (*Brief pause*) One hundred and seventy years ago. (*Brief pause*) I'm not the most brilliant banker in Moscow. Have you been to Oreanda?

ANNA   Sorry?

GUROV   Oreanda — the waterfall. Almost an hour from here. Well worth a visit. There's a train every —

> *He breaks off suddenly, leans into her and speaks very softly, almost conspiratorially.*

Don't look now; but there's a young man over there on your right. Pink cravat, white shoes. See him?

ANNA   Yes?

GUROV   Watch what he's slipping into his coffee.

ANNA   Sugar?

GUROV   Liquid heroin.

ANNA   He's not!

GUROV   Don't stare.

ANNA   How do you — ?

GUROV   Had to be taken down from the top of the cathedral spire last Sunday. Before Vespers. They say his wife ran off last month with a cavalry officer.

ANNA   God!

GUROV   One-armed. Tragic story. And do you see that frail little creature in the satin dress — looks as if she's about to die?

ANNA   Where?

GUROV   No. Further left.

ANNA   The black dress?

GUROV   She's in charge of the elephants in the Moscow zoo.

ANNA   That little white-haired lady with the — ?

GUROV   And the husband, the enormous man with the grey beard? (*Examines his nails*) He knows you're talking about him.

ANNA   I'm not —

GUROV   (*Loudly*) They expect some rain this afternoon. But it is that time of year, isn't it? (*Softly again*) At least twenty-five stone weight. Too much brandy. Once the principal dancer at the Kirov.

ANNA   That man was a ballet — ?

GUROV   Known in those days as Il Folletto. The Elf. Italian. She's German. They got married while they were still at college — just like me. And each has refused to learn the other's language; so that when they want to communicate, they write notes to one another.

ANNA   They don't!

GUROV   In broken English.

ANNA   I think you're trying to make a —

GUROV   Look. She's passing him a message now.

ANNA   So she is.

GUROV   He's reading it. Shakes his head. Disapproves of whatever it is she has said. Passes it back to her.

ANNA   Yes.

GUROV   Strange way to talk, isn't it?

ANNA   Wait a minute — !

GUROV   Eventually their vocal chords will atrophy.

ANNA That's the bill she handed him! (*Laughs*) Their coffee bill!

GUROV (*Innocently*) Is it?

ANNA Yes! She's putting her money on top of it!

GUROV You're absolutely right.

ANNA You are taking a hand at me!

GUROV No, no. Just playing the Yalta game.

ANNA The what?

GUROV I'll explain it later. I'm going to Oreanda tomorrow to say goodbye to the waterfall. Come with me.

ANNA Oh, I couldn't —

GUROV And bring the charming lady along and we'll baptise her up there in the silver water. What will we call her?

ANNA My husband will make that —

GUROV Yalta! What about Yalta?

ANNA A dog called Yalta?

GUROV Why not? Always remind you of here. By the way I'm Dmitry Gurov. From Moscow. And you are — ?

ANNA I . . . I'm Anna Sergeyevna. From Pargolovo.

GUROV Italian?

ANNA (*Laughs*) Pargolovo is thirty miles west of Petersburg.

GUROV Pargolovo? It's three miles south of Rome. I think in real life you're a tenor in an Italian opera company. We get a lot of them in Moscow. (*Softly*) See that man eating an ice-cream? He claims to be an illegitimate son of Queen Victoria of England. He's probably right. She had nineteen. (*Loudly*) I'll pick you up at the Marino at ten and I'll have you safely home in time for dinner. You never got your coffee!

He jumps to his feet.

17

ANNA **It doesn't matter.**

GUROV **Maybe the coffee waiters are on a coffee break. I'll find out.** Would she turn up? Perhaps. With her cranky little mongrel. And if she doesn't . . . ? (*He shrugs indifferently*)

ANNA What a strange man. One hundred and seventy! (*Laughs*) Forty, maybe? And married? Said so, didn't he? Probably two or three children. Could be grown up by now. Not a bit like a banker — or a philologist; whatever a philologist looks like. Should ask him that. Happy nature? Not sure. For all his joking there's something . . . urgent about him.

GUROV Curious word, 'conquest', isn't it? 'I made another conquest last night.' Militaristic ring about it; maybe even a hint of violence. I'm not squeamish about it but it's a word I never used. I suppose because I've never thought of the women I've had over the years as trophies. More like companions in adventure — exciting adventures — delightful companions — light-hearted, soufflé adventures. Yes. That's how it always begins. It's an unacknowledged game, too. Of course it can become complicated; and then a bit difficult; and then maybe even a little frightening; and that's when you resolve never to become entangled again. But the beginning is always . . . joyous. And who can resist that? Why should it be resisted? (*Loudly*) **Isn't it an impressive waterfall?**

ANNA **What?**

GUROV (*Shouts*) **Isn't it wonderful?**

ANNA **Yes.**

GUROV **It looks silver, doesn't it?**

ANNA **It's frightening.**

GUROV **A thousand gallons of water crash down**

there every thirty seconds.

ANNA It's a bit overwhelming.

GUROV Where's Yalta? (*To dog*) Come here and see this. (*To* ANNA) She's frightened by the noise. And she's not dying about me. (*Softly*) Nor I about her. (*To* ANNA) Let's move back a bit. When is your husband going to join you?

ANNA As soon as he can get away.

GUROV Away from what?

ANNA His work.

GUROV What's his work?

ANNA He's a clerical officer in the office of the district council — I'm wrong — in the municipal office. (*Laughs*) One or the other. Isn't it awful — I'm never sure which.

GUROV Shame on you. Anyhow, if he comes before I leave, we'll have to bring him up here.

ANNA You're leaving tomorrow, aren't you?

GUROV I think I'll stay on for another few days. We haven't explored the gardens. Haven't been to the casino. And on Friday night we're going to meet the Theodosia ferry. (*Suddenly very softly*) D'you see that barefoot boy at the railings? Beside the woman in the green shawl? He has just lifted her purse from her handbag.

ANNA How do you — ? (*She slaps his arm playfully*) Will you stop that! Come on. We'll miss the train.

GUROV Thank you for coming with me today.

ANNA Yalta — Yalta — come on, girl — come on.

GUROV Who are you calling?

ANNA Yalta! We have just baptised her! My dog!

GUROV What dog?

ANNA My dog. There.

GUROV (*Slaps her arm playfully*) Will you stop that! You know there's no dog there.

19

ANNA At your feet. There. Touch her. You are a
     very silly man.

GUROV Yes.

ANNA We're going to miss the train.

GUROV The next day we explored the municipal
      gardens. The following night we went to the
      casino where I swaggered a little — stupidly;
      and lost more than a little. She was . . .
      prudent. And two days later, on the Friday
      night, we went down to the harbour and
      watched the arrival of the Theodosia ferry
      with its lights dancing and expectant.

ANNA Why did I think he was strange? He wasn't at
      all strange. Just an ordinary man. And con-
      siderate. And generous. And funny! God! He
      would say something altogether absurd and
      you would look at him and his face would be
      almost solemn. I hadn't laughed so much in
      years. And yet at times he would withdraw
      into himself and you felt that — what? I don't
      know — you knew there was a great lone-
      liness in him.

GUROV I had never seen her so at ease or so happy as
      that night at the harbour. Or indeed so beauti-
      ful; with that unique beauty that youth endows.
      And in front of all those new, expectant
      arrivals we kissed. Yes. Without embarrass-
      ment. Then I took her hand and we went back
      to the Marino Hotel and up to her room.
      (*Pause*) It has to be said that she locked the
      damn dog in the closet and the bastard
      scratched at the door all night long. It has to
      be said, too, that the next morning was . . .
      turbulent. Tears. Regrets. Contrition. The usual.
      She actually did say, 'You'll be the first not to
      respect me now.' Just a little disappointing.

ANNA (*Crying*) Why should you? How could you?

You picked me up in the square, didn't you?

GUROV Anna, you —

ANNA To you I'm just another street woman. How many more have you had since you came here?

GUROV I have the utmost respect for you.

ANNA And what you know nothing about and of course care nothing about is that I'm married to the most wonderful man who is kind and honourable and adores me.

GUROV Why wouldn't he?

ANNA And I have betrayed that honourable man and I have degraded myself.

GUROV Anna —

ANNA What I have done is so wrong — no, not wrong, evil, evil. I am an evil person.

GUROV Shhh.

ANNA If you could see your eyes: you despise me and you're right to despise me. Oh my God, why did I ever set foot in this corrupt place!

GUROV And the emotion was genuine. Completely. Maybe a shade . . . theatrical. But no question of fakery. The poor child did think she had become — thankfully she didn't use the words but they wouldn't have been inappropriate to the way she was feeling — 'a fallen woman'. Yes. Remarkable.

ANNA (*Calmly*) All I could see were Nikolai's quiet, earnest eyes, those beautiful earnest eyes. They weren't accusing; weren't even reproachful. They just gazed at me and asked, 'Why, Anna? Why?'

GUROV Then she threw her arms around me and hugged me fiercely as if I could rescue her from herself. And I noticed how lank her hair hung round her face and how those pert little features had gone so slack. And I realised suddenly that she was only a few years older than my daughter.

ANNA I wanted so much to feel him hold me and hear him say in that gentle voice of his, 'Anna, my infant, my infant'. I needed that assurance so badly.

GUROV We got through that morning somehow. Of course I told her I loved her, as indeed I did. And finally the sobbing stopped and the fear went out of her eyes and somehow I even coaxed a laugh from her. Then we had lunch in Verner's Restaurant — mussels with garlic stuffing, done in a white wine. We both had the same. Excellent. Then a pleasant walk along the promenade. Had we had an established routine, you could have said we were back to normal.

She takes his arm and leans into him and speaks very softly, almost conspiratorially.

ANNA **Look at the pair across the street. Don't stare! See them?**

GUROV **I see them. And that's my role.**

ANNA **Where is his left hand?**

GUROV **What?**

ANNA **His left hand — where is it? — can you see it?**

GUROV **I see a man in a grey —**

ANNA **But no left hand visible. And why not?**

GUROV **I see a staid couple enjoying a brisk —**

ANNA **The beast! Oh my God! In broad daylight!**

GUROV **What are you talking — ?**

ANNA **She's trying to walk normally, but how can she? God!**

GUROV **Are you telling me he's — ?**

She whispers quickly into GUROV's *ear — then explodes with laughter. He laughs too, and stares at her in pretended shock and amazement.*

Well, aren't you a naughty child!
ANNA **I swear!**
GUROV **Very naughty.**
ANNA **But I'm right, amn't I?**
GUROV **Absolutely!**
ANNA **Look at her face! And the beast believes that if he keeps looking away from her, then nobody could guess what —**

Again she leans into him to whisper a further comment; but breaks off suddenly in panic.

Yalta! Oh my God! Dmitry —
GUROV **What?**
ANNA **Where's Yalta?**
GUROV **Isn't she there at — ?**
ANNA **She's gone!**
GUROV **She's not gone. We'll stand —**
ANNA **Oh God, my darling birthday present.**

She begins calling the dog and dashing frantically around.

Yalta! Yalta! Where is she? Oh God, Dmitry — she's been stolen — she's lost — she's run away! Yalta! Where are you? Yalta? You weren't watching her!
GUROV **She can't be lost, Anna.**
ANNA **Where is she then? Yalta!**
GUROV **She must be around here somewhere.**
ANNA **You know she's not. Why didn't you mind her? Yalta! She's wise — she'll head for**

home. She is wise, isn't she? She'll go home to the Marino. Don't stand there, Dmitry! You keep an eye on the far side of the street and I'll search this side. Oh my God, what will I tell Nikolai if she's not in the hotel, if I have lost her?

GUROV She was right: the wise Yalta had made her way home. There she was up in the bedroom, sitting possessively on the bed.

ANNA *whips the dog up into her arms.*

ANNA Oh my darling, darling, darling dog! Kiss me — kiss me. And again and again! (*To* GUROV) Look at how wretched she is. (*To dog*) You're right to be ashamed of yourself. But all is forgiven, forgotten, my little sweetheart. Kiss her, Dmitry — yes, kiss Dmitry, my darling. And never run away from me again — d'you hear? Never! Never! Look at that little tail wagging like mad. Isn't she just beautiful?

GUROV (*Looking at* ANNA) Yes. Indeed, yes. Very beautiful. Happiness all over the place.

So we pulled over the curtains and didn't go out again until it was time for dinner. And this time we were circumspect: we didn't lock the beast in the closet.

ANNA You're early. I didn't expect you for another hour.

GUROV I've got a cab waiting at the door. This morning we'll go across to Alushta to see the old Byzantine church there. It has the finest mosaic dome in the Crimea.

ANNA I've just got a telegram from Nikolai.

GUROV From — ?

ANNA Nikolai. My husband. He has to go into

hospital. A serious eye infection. He wants me to come home immediately. He sounds frightened.

GUROV Ah.

ANNA So I'm taking the overnight express.

GUROV Of course.

ANNA Tonight.

GUROV Yes.

ANNA Just as well I'm going, isn't it?

GUROV Yes?

ANNA Nikolai being sent to hospital — people call that fate, don't they? Will you see me off?

GUROV When does the train leave?

ANNA Seven-thirty.

GUROV Of course I'll see you off.

ANNA It is all for the best, isn't it?

GUROV (*On the train, briskly*) I think that's everything. The bed seems comfortable and the place is warm. Not too warm, is it? Your cases are up there. Where's your hatbox?

She holds up an imaginary box.

Good. Yalta can sleep on that mat. And there's your coffee-flask and croissants. And should you decide in the middle of the night that you don't want to see Pargolovo for another few days — I still think you made that up —

ANNA What?

GUROV Pargolovo.

ANNA That's where I live, Dmitry.

GUROV So you say. But even if you do, it's in Italy. You're going in the wrong direction.

ANNA Thirty miles west of Petersburg.

GUROV Sorry. Three miles south of Rome. Check when you get there. Anyhow I was going to say that should you decide during the night that you don't want to go to Italy, pull that cord, and —

ANNA Just look at me for a moment, Dmitry, and let me look at you. (*Pause*) No, don't kiss me, please. You know I'm never going to see you again — ever.

GUROV Anna —

ANNA But I will always love you — always.

GUROV And I will always —

ANNA Shhh. You don't have to make any declarations. Really. It would have been better if we had never met. Indeed it would. But we did meet and now my life can never be the same again. There's the second bell. Go, Dmitry. (*He moves towards her*) No, please, darling, please, please . . . 'Bye.

She turns away quickly.

GUROV The night had turned chilly and the platform soon emptied but I felt I ought to stand there until the train was out of sight. Express trains take a very long time to build up speed, I discovered. I hadn't my gloves with me and my hands were quite cold. And my feet. Autumn had arrived. The season was certainly over. What did I feel? As if I had woken up; emerged from a sweet trance; returned from another charming adventure. A light-hearted adventure — it was that indeed. With a very sweet adventuress. And all the more agreeable because it had come to an end before the complications began and things became difficult. That was always a bonus.

But already in my mind that texture of the thing was changing. The little adventure —

how long did it last? — a week? — ten days?
— however real it may have seemed at the
time, it was already losing that reality and
beginning to drift into the category of . . .
'imagined'. But there was always something
elusive, something impalpable about it, wasn't
there? Did it happen at all? I began to think —
truthfully! — I began to wonder had I made it
all up!

Maybe it was not more actual than the
fictional lives I invested the people in the
square with.

He warms to this intriguing speculation.

Now this was a subtle game, sly almost. There
is no silver waterfall at Oreanda.

What?

None. And there never was a Marino Hotel.

You're joking.

The Theodosia ferry was a ghost ship. No
municipal park; no promenade; no town
square.

No town square?

All a fiction. All imagined.

Oh come on!

Was there even — could it be thought even
in a sly game — was there ever an Anna?

Oh, God, shame on you!

But was there?

That's unfair to her and to you.

Is it?

Of course there was an Anna, a beautiful
Anna, an exciting Anna, even though it does
require a little effort to recall that excitement.
And that's unfair too. You remember that
excitement well. You remember that excite-

ment very well indeed . . . well, don't you? So no more of that cheap game, that ugly game.

You're right.

You're a callous bastard, you know that?

I do know that.

So just shut up.

Very well.

But there was one element I was happy to consign to the imagined. The damned dog was definitely make-believe. Definitely never any Yalta.

ANNA Nikolai was a month in hospital. Then, when he came out, he got an infection in the other eye and had to go back in again. So for nine weeks I was alone in the house with Sonia, the maid. It was a bleak time. The snow had come early. It was almost an hour's walk to the hospital every day. And I was anxious about Nikolai because he was worrying himself sick about his job and about money but most of all in case those quiet, earnest eyes might lose their sight altogether. I had to keep assuring him that they wouldn't. He had become so dependant on me, as if we had switched roles. He usually cried when visiting time was over. Dmitry was with me all the time. But his presence had different manifestations and different levels of intensity. Sometimes I wouldn't see him for days; only the echo of his voice; and I'd strain to hear was he calling me. Or maybe a quick memory of the way he'd pronounce 'Theodosia' or summon a waiter — 'When you find a second'. Sometimes I could hear him moving around upstairs and I'd wait at the bottom of the stairs for him to come down. Sometimes he sat at the far side of the stove, reading a novel or doing his bank books; and when he remembered me, he'd look across at me and smile quickly. And sometimes he'd come up behind me stealthily and enfold me in his arms and whisper into the back of my neck, just below the hairline. And when he did that, I was flooded with such a great happiness that I would have collapsed if he had let me go.

It was a strange kind of living; knowing with an aching clarity that I would never see him again — ever; and at the same time being with him always, always, happily always in that ethereal presence. There were times when I thought I mightn't be right in the head. But I suppose what was happening to me was that I was becoming somebody altogether different.

GUROV Something peculiar happened to me over the next two months. Moscow had become intolerable — Moscow that I loved. And the work in the bank was so meaningless that I had to frogmarch myself through the routine of every day. Found myself doing things I would never have done, just to escape from the house and the sullen silence and the children demanding help with their homework. I joined a tennis club! In November! Played cards three nights a week. Accompanied a colleague to his weekly musical society evenings and endured his amateur friends playing Bach and Handel. With such enthusiasm! And with apparent pleasure, for God's sake!

But back to the peculiar thing, the very peculiar thing. Remember my sly game? Well, it . . . inverted itself. Or else my world did a somersault. Or else all reality turned itself on

29

its head. Because suddenly, for no reason that I was aware of, things that once seemed real now became imagined things. And what was imagined, what I could imagine, what I could recall, that was actual, the only actuality. The bank, colleagues, home, card games, they all subsided into make-believe — they were fictions, weren't they? And the only reality was the reality in my mind. And that was the reality of the Marino Hotel and the silver waterfall and the town square which was the heart of Yalta. And, of course, the total reality of Anna.

So I began to live only in her presence, only in the environment that was hers. In the whisper of her breath. In the music of her laugh. In the balm of her voice. In the solace of her hands. So that when I knew in mid-December that I had to go to Pargolovo, it wasn't an impetuous decision. It was the most natural thing in the world to do.

ANNA I began to fill my weeks with small delights, exquisite little treats. Well, expectations really. And I plotted them with great care, indeed with cunning. It wasn't at all a game, a child's make-believe. No, no. It was a rehearsal for what was certainly going to happen.

On Friday afternoon, when Nikolai has gone for his check-up and Sonia is down at the laundry, at exactly four o'clock there'll be a knock at the door. Three crisp taps. I'll have a quick look in the hall mirror and then I'll open it. And there he'll be, with his straw hat and his quirky smile and he'll say, 'Will you get a move on? The ferry's about to leave.'

And on Saturday week next, on my way to the butcher, we'll meet at noon under the town clock. Ever since I came to Pargolovo the hands have been frozen at ten; and he'll say, 'Look at that, Anna. You're two years late, for God's sake.'

And in tomorrow's post there'll be a letter from him. I'll tell Nikolai it's from my sister, Irena. It will have all the plans for our elopement to the Crimea and the house we'll have there and the whitewashed rooms and the sea-blue dishes on the dresser and the trees we'll plant and the walks we'll take. He knows blue is my favourite colour.

Yes. They were rehearsals.

The three taps didn't come. No rat-tat-tat. And he wasn't waiting under the frozen clock. And there was no letter about the sea-blue dishes. But those weren't big disappointments. Weren't disappointments at all. Only postponements of the complete happiness that had to come.

He grabs her from behind. She is alarmed and totally confused.

GUROV **Anna.**
ANNA **What? — Who? —**
GUROV **Isn't it Anna Sergeyevna?**

She wheels around and sees him.

ANNA **Oh my God!** (*Pause. Softly*) **Oh my God.**
GUROV **I had to come.**
ANNA **Dmitry?**
GUROV **Dmitry — yes.**
ANNA **Oh my God.**
GUROV (*Rapidly*) **I found out where you lived and I went to the house but I couldn't knock so I**

walked the streets for the past three hours in the hope that I would see you and I did, I did, I couldn't believe it, but there you were —

ANNA You've got to go.

GUROV (*Slowly*) Looking exactly as I knew you would — no, more beautiful. Much, much more beautiful —

ANNA What are you doing here? Listen to me! You can't stay! For God's sake, go!

GUROV And your skin smells the same and your hands and —

ANNA Where are you staying?

GUROV Where am I what?

ANNA Staying — staying! How long have you been here?

GUROV I'm in the Railway Hotel.

ANNA Oh God, this is awful. I knew I'd never see you again. I knew that.

GUROV But I'm here.

ANNA I'm out to buy paraffin.

GUROV Look at me.

ANNA We need paraffin for the bedroom lamp.

GUROV Look at me, Anna.

ANNA When are you leaving?

GUROV I'm going to kiss you.

ANNA The street is full! You've gone mad!

GUROV Just once.

ANNA People — people, for God's sake, Dmitry. No, no, please, Dmitry — go now — please go now before —

GUROV Only once.

ANNA You can't — you can't! People everywhere. Please, Dmitry. I'll come to you in Moscow next —

GUROV Just one kiss.

ANNA Oh my God — Moscow, that's a promise — oh my darling —

She throws her arms around him and kisses him quickly.

I must go — Moscow, I swear — I'll write to you at the bank — it'll be early next month — oh my love, my love —

She kisses him again, holding his face in her hands.

I'm going now — oh my God, Dmitry —
GUROV **And you're right about Pargolovo.**

She stares blankly at him — what is he talking about?

ANNA **Am I?**
GUROV **It isn't in Italy.**
ANNA **Yes.**
GUROV **No. It is in Russia.**
ANNA **Is it?**
GUROV **It's here.**
ANNA **Oh my God.**
GUROV **I was wrong.**
ANNA **No, no — Moscow — a promise. I swear, my love.**
GUROV **Moscow.**

She turns away quickly.

ANNA I went to him in Moscow every two or three months. As often as I could. Nikolai believed I was going to see a gynaecologist. I would check into the hotel and send a porter around to the bank with a message that I had arrived. 'Il Folletto is in town.' — That was our code. Dmitry's idea. Just a joke. And he would come to me that night. And in the morning I would go back to Pargolovo. (*Suddenly remembering*) Yes, Nikolai's eyesight improved a lot — well, got no worse. He wore dark glasses all the time and went for long walks with Yalta. And to make his job easier his superior switched him from municipal work to district council work — or from district council work to — (*Impatiently*) whatever. Their concern for him . . . flattered him. I think he just pretended to believe in the gynaecologist.

GUROV I had never led a double life before and it was surprising how simple it was — at one level. My public life continued as usual: work, acquaintances, family, clients, holidays; fully conventional; altogether transparent; and a total deception.

Then there was the other life with her: tempestuous, ecstatic, tortured and thrilling in its secrecy. That life took over my entire being and gripped me in its mad eddy. This is my true life, I thought, and in a way it was.

But of course these categories — public and private, deceptive and authentic — they are never as distinct as we think. Because the authentic life has its own little deceits within it and the deceptive life has its own little authenticities. And the two categories bleed into each other. So that a time can come when you can barely distinguish between them. I didn't think that was a confusion on my part. Just an acknowledgement of things as they are. And I did love her. Oh yes. I had never loved anyone like that before.

Why are you crying?

ANNA **Give me a moment.**

He takes her in his arms.

GUROV **Shhh.**

ANNA **Can't stop. Just stupid.**

GUROV **There's a special perfume off your hair tonight.**

ANNA **Our lives are in ruins, Dmitry.**

GUROV **Why are you so upset today?**

ANNA **We hide from everyone. We lie all the time. We live like fugitives.**

GUROV **You are such a beautiful fugitive.**

ANNA **And we're never going to escape. How can we? Neither of us is ever going to be free. And I love you so much, so much. No, I don't just love you — I worship you. Oh, Dmitry, my darling, you will love me always, won't you?**

GUROV **She believed she did worship me. She believed she would always worship me. And for the first time in my life I had come close to worshipping somebody too. But how could I tell her that this would come to an end one day? Indeed it would. But if I had told her, she wouldn't have believed me.**

> *He releases her. They stand back-to-back, facing in opposite directions, holding hands.*

ANNA **You will love me always, Dmitry?**

GUROV **Yes.**

ANNA **And I will love you always.**

GUROV **I know that.**

ANNA **We are so lucky. Do you appreciate how lucky we are? How many people do you know have had such happiness as we have had? We have been such a . . . blessed couple, haven't we?**

GUROV **Yes.**

ANNA **I do believe that. Blessed.**

GUROV **Yes.**

ANNA At moments like that — and we had so many, so many of them — at moments like that I was convinced we would find a solution to our predicament. No, not a solution — why not a divine intervention? Yes, a miraculous solution would be offered to us. And that release would make our happiness so complete and so opulent and . . . forever. But I knew that until that miracle happened, we would have to stumble on together for a very long time; because the end was coming even though it was still a long way off. But the drawing to a close had already begun and we were now embarked on the most complicated and most frightening and the most painful time of all.

GUROV **Kiss me, Anna. Please.**

They kiss. Bring up the exuberant military music in the background.